Erotic Expressions

&

Intimate Episodes

SpitVerb Entertainment LLC

Copyright © 2008, 2013 by Jamelle Davenport
All rights reserved. This book, or parts thereof,
May not be reproduced in any form whatsoever
unless permission is received from author and/or
representative.
ISBN: 978-0-6151-7325-2

Erotic Expressions

CONTENTS

Erotic Expressions & Intimate Episodes

I. Erotic Expressions

1. Touching Me
2. Lunch
3. Outside
4. Supper (thought)
5. Smooth (thought)
6. Supper
7. Jewels in My Cushion Box
8. Never Let Me Go
9. The Porno (from a lonely man's point of view)
10. Horny (from a lonely man's point of view)
11. I Feel Hot
12. The Experience

II. Intimate Episodes

13. Perfection
14. Pussy
15. Breast
16. So Little
17. She Speaks of a Good Kiss
18. Tender Touch
19. Sensual
20. Sing Lovers
21. I Dream
22. Valentine I (from a man's point of view)

23. **Valentine II (from a woman's point of view)**
24. **Tickles in the Middle**
25. **Sizzling**
26. **He Speaks of a Good Kiss**
27. **Proposal**
28. **Woman (from a man's point of view)**
29. **Heated (from a lonely man's point of view)**
30. **Fetishes**

About Author

Intimate Episodes

CHAPTER 1
Erotic Expressions

Touching Me

Touching

Caressing

Kissing

Teasing

It feels so good

Knees weak

Nipples wrinkle

Stomach grumbles

I am not hungry

Body is dancing all over him

I cannot make it stop

The sensations

The temptation

I want it

He wants it

Sucking

Groping

Licking

Stroking

Soaking wet

Very wet

Sliding all between

Gliding in and out

Heart is pounding
I cannot breathe
There is light in my eyes
I see the light it is so bright
Your fingertips inside my womanhood playing my strings

Lunch

This home is quiet
I am all alone
Should I make my own noise?
Talking to myself, is out of the question
So let me stop now
I need you now
Now I need you
I want what I have missed
Sitting here on the edge of the bed massaging mine own thighs
Naked thighs
Licking mine own lips
Titillating mine own nipples with the tips of my fingers
Gyratory
On the edge of the bed

I missed brunch how about lunch?
That is just a fantasy
I know that you are busy
It's raining outside, I can see it against my window
I am raining outside; I feel the lubrication on my own flesh, wetting in between my fingers
Sitting here thinking of you
Of us two and the things we could do
If you were here
I will just follow the weather
Until my lily is pumping against my palm like thunder
Like thunder traveling beneath my skin
Deep within like an unguided tickle
When the orgasm is unleashed
I will inhale a longing scent from my own fingers until I fall asleep
I miss you

Outside

Mannequin: Place her in a display window
In a wall to wall box standing there in one position
Half dressed in designer lingerie
Breast lifted and firm
Nipples hard and protruding
They will gawk at her from the outside
Cover model: Place her on a magazine cover
Flat and paper thin
They are outside looking in
At the camera light glowing across her naked body
The airstream of the fan blowing in her hair
Legs spread apart and nothing covers her there
It is open for the world to see
They will glare at her from the outside
Hip hop model: Place her in a music video
Where she is labeled as a ho
Shaking her rear end for the cameramen
Slow and fast
Round and round
Up and down
It must be the ass because she is definitely out of

place
Dancing on top of tables perspiring between her breast
Batting her fake eyelashes with hair weave clinging to her face
At least she doesn't have to take off her clothes
They will gawp at her from the outside
Stripper: Faint smell of old beer comes from their breath
For them intoxication brings fascination
A throbbing erection of impatient blood vessels wanting some stimulation
They imagine stretching her womanhood inside and out
The tighter the better, not for her pleasure but for their own pleasures
To torment her womanhood
Sliding through labial lips, where it is soft, wet and warm
A perfect rendezvous
Wishing the girl at home was her
Perfect with no voice
Now dance on his body
Hips up close to his face

He wants to smell it, he wants to lick it and play in that misused place
A jovial, swinging scrotum hardening inside his pants
As he stands, stares and fantasizes
He is ejaculating
Eyes squinting, off balance, a bit dizzy
His erection droops back into its folds lazily
Then he will be on his way
The next man waits
He will stare at her from the outside

Supper (thought)

Appetizing
Licking my lips
Crossing my legs
Food is not a necessity for what I am longing

Smooth (thought)

Tasting
Warm and moist
Smooth like Chap Stick
Nakedness

Supper

She sat there thinking- The sheer beauty of that man

His baby fine skin

The plumpness in his lips

The way his jaws moved as he ate

The strong flexing in his chest heaving as he talked

Tight hard muscles

All over his body

Protruding beneath his shirt

Gritting teeth

Temples carved into his face

He sat there thinking- His blood is pumping feverishly

Thinking of his hard arms holding unto her

Releasing in her

She tasting his nakedness

With her glossed lips against

His throbbing skin

Surely, the taste for this plate of supper is lost

His senses connecting to something more appetizing

Her senses connecting to something more

appetizing

A hunger both want to feed

She thought- Four years of waiting for a man's touch

He thought- One year of flirting for a woman's touch

The thought brings forth a chuckle

A naughty smile his way

A wink her way

She sat there thinking- She is envisioning his masculine body naked

Lavishing her dewy flower with friction

Her little swollen flesh is enjoying the thought

To shudder to that unreachable tickle

Feeling that liquid stream flow between

Excitement

Letting loose a long lusty cry of delight

Her hot spongy flesh in discontent

Like a boat lost at sea

He sat there thinking- And he can see

That she is willing and wanting

He throws in the napkin

To signal a reaction

From her

Licking his lips and imagining the taste of that wine dissolved in her system
All for him to ponder
Her symphony in his opera
His conducting strokes will be known
Because he is taking her home

Jewel in my cushion box

He sleeps like a man
Arms across his chest rising with every breath
One leg bent the other out
His manhood sprouting
His smooth stomach loving the tickles of the open air
His serenity is handsome
He is handsome
I snuggle close
Under his throat
His hard muscular back
Sideways on the sack
I tug at the tight covers wrapped around his body
I wrap my legs around his waist
A feel

Erotic Expressions

A sensation

Of his warmth

His hot breath rolling on the curve of my breast

A tickle

A sliver of saliva

Here and there

My nipples hurt from observation

I have wet the sheets in anticipation

My sap is leaking like a Maple tree

Intoxicated with

His fetching way of sleeping

I am unable to sleep

Feeling nonexistent in this twilight hour

Me alone in my insomniac refuge

The bright full night eye in the sky

Cast a shadow to share my bed

A bright shadowy companion to warm the

threads in which I would normally lay

Next to my man

Another reason to want to feel him

All of him

This sculpture

Every perfect

Erotic

Detail

Of his landscape

Running my fingers south through his soft pubic hair

Le massage et attire his sex in my palm

A strong tickle inside my anatomy slips away

In a lonely haste

His genital is limp and

My hormones are speaking

My womanhood is screaming

Roll!

Get out!

Of the bed, my disappointed hormones said

Tiptoe

Tip

Tiptoe

Away

I inset myself in the love seat to fall asleep

(Breath sounds)

My breathing swallowed up the night

No dreams

No solitude

The early morning hours slowly crept in

Bringing the sunshine in

Erotic Expressions

My eyes a bit bright with the early rise of the red sunlight
Squinting and stretching I looked ahead and there he stood in front of me
A sight to see
My handsome man
Naked
Aroused and watching me
As I had done he
The red sunset bouncing off his flesh
Whiny my voice in the interior of my throat
Like a kitten I purred
My breath stale like old peppermint
No speaking
My choice
My man
Delivers
Soft kisses to my neck
He gloats at my flesh
Hungry man
Horny man
Mmm
Whispering his naughty desires in my bosom
My womanhood wetting like spring dribbles on

the grass
I drift into him like cautious fog
Submissively
I answer to his sexual call
His strong hands guiding me
His arms turning me around
To face away
Then I frown
I wish I had a peppermint
Cradling my breast in his hands
Fondling
Squeezing
Teasing
Pulling at
My nipples wickedly
Grabbing my buttocks cheeks between his teeth
He worships my backside with dainty kisses
Lubricating his hardness between the flesh
His pulsating erection thumping against the curve
Of my backside
Stimulating his artery
His fingers began to
Slowly stir

Erotic Expressions

In and out of me
Wet and silky
Like music to my ears
His waist dancing against my backside
Spreading my legs wide
His fingers dripping wet with sweet juices
Penetrating
Penetrating
Into my hot wet flesh
My man
His scrotum
I squeeze it all
As he pulls me back
I tickle that sac
Bouncing off my walls
Slamming up and down my back
The friction in my crack
Widening my hips I spread apart my vaginal lips
To give it
All
To him
Deeper
Into my contracting muscles
Deeper

Deeper

Bending

Body

Yoga

Karate vaginally on his male jewel

I'm going crazy

Feeling him jolt with surprise

His throat growl

Hugging me hard and close

His jewel beating a place deep in my cushion box

Handsome he is

Savage beauty is his duty

I listen to his heart thumping in his chest

As if it is the bass in the music, we dance to

His breaths are restless

Sweaty air

Sweet as rum

Steam rising from our pores

Stuck tight

Like bubble gum

I want more

So much more

His hardness gets weak

Slippery

Erotic Expressions

Sliding

Just when I feel so sweet

(Sigh)

Just when I feel so high

So deep and resigned

The sliver of the tickle blowing out my high

His ego depressing from my unease

He slows his progression for a tease

Sucking on my skin

Teasing the best of me

He sacrifices his selfish pleasure for unity

And churns the mixture with the fullness of his tongue

He licked and spit

Suckled and spit

Until

I did an involuntary split

Shaking and

Writhing in an orgasmic conclusion

Never Let Me Go

Knock, knock

Come in, it is open!

Enter a room and set it on fire

With lust and desire a heat wave is coming and the elements are not ready

For this not so steady not even monogamous

Just sex and fulfillment

Composing moans of odd ranges

Secretions of warm lubricants

Sweaty bodies

Gliding

Colliding

Molding mounds of flesh

Position after position

Changing like the pages of a tantric scroll

In addition, to the belly rolls

Something sweet and edible

Never let me go

Never let me go

The filling of that cavity- not on the teeth- digging in it deep

Reaching for that soft interior with raging

Who says the sea is deep some parts are but

shallow
We can go there and wade with our bodies
Where the sun rest at the edges coming out
slowly just for a tease and back again fast and
forceful
Await the grasp

The Porno
(From a lonely man's point of view)

Sitting here watching a porno
No feelings of guilt
My desperate act alone
Exciting
Tiring
Depressing
So much to raise my senses
Although I wish it were real
I wish the hands groping my dick were the soft
hands of a woman
I wished that I were the man on the screen
indulging myself like syrup all over
Those
Soft

Moving beauties
Perfect in all the right places
Nipples like the ones on bottles
Fantasizing about the two girls giggling on my television screen
The porno is still playing
My hands motionless on my throne
The porno never escaping my sight
The television flashing colorful lights on my abdominal hairs
Two girls licking each other's bodies on my television screen
My hands pulling at my pubic hairs
My out of shape thighs opening and closing
My eyelids are wilting with thoughts
Two girls
Soft, bodacious and smiling at me through my television screen
Perfume flaring on the hard walls of my nostrils
My head is falling back to hit the full pillows of the couch cushions
Two girls
Pink flesh, brown flesh, wet, pubic shaven, flat bellies

Intimate Episodes

Erotic Expressions

My throbbing vessel attentive

Hold her

Yes, hold her too

Play with them

Yes, play

The pink is playing with her brown and rare

Seasoned juices

Chocolate like areas

Soft laughter surrounds my heightened libido

Girlish laughter

Playful and squeaky

Mischievously stroking my genital

Pressing little soft fingers

Rubbing up and down my shaft

Pulling my nipples in between their teeth

Licking my ears

Release, release

So damn sweet

Pinching, pushing, pulling

Their lips appreciate my tender sac

Hardening it

Making my hips twitch

My toes tingle

Twirling my erection across succulent lips

Teasing me sweet with their tongues

My hips take a ride

Lean wet thighs

Desperate eyes

Passive surprise

Hopping and riding

Taking turns

Squeezing their hot flesh all over it

Like a drug that will not quit

Is this a dream or the porno?

Intimate Episodes

Erotic Expressions

Horny

(From a lonely man's point of view)

I am so horny
I could cry 'til dry puddles form on my cheeks
I just want to spread my hairy thighs and cry
Wiggle my toes, stretch my back, and reminisce
Let my erect stroke stand tall and wobble against
the cold air
Just to dream of a woman's warm and wet,
caress on my sensitive mushroomed top
I am so horny
Hugging and kissing my pillows
Fantasizing," Do me baby!"
My stomach muscles contracting at the thought
Soft, warm and wet
Sweet tasting
Sweet smelling
Sweet looking
Save the kisses for after
I am so horny
Baby wherever you are
You blow my mind

I Feel Hot

I just want to fuck
All...night...long
I want the dick and balls up as far as my gut
Let me be bowlegged by morning
So the essence of your presence is showing
Come here handsome, wrap my body into a knot, and give me everything you got
Do not let the screaming stop you
My bodies shaking halt you
Continue the motion until you feel the warm potion wanting an exit
STOP!
Give me some kisses
Slap that ass a little and watch the color change
Stay in the mind frame of the fucking game
We got another journey and it is not love making its lust taking a ride
It is the passion for that dick
That long, strong and thick...
Caress and taunt it
Thump it across that clit and plunge in it
Keep rising between my thighs
Let your thrust be like thunder

**The deeper the stroke the more I choke with every moan
'Cause I just want to fuck
I just want to fuck
All...night...long**

The Experience

Yesterday morning I felt on top of the world
Like a new girl
Closed in for so long it was time to take an adventure
I thought to myself; let my soul experience freedom for it is starved
Fantasizing all day, I begged myself to be loose, not so protective, have fun, and give in to my desires
Give me this naked man as I see him in my head
Let me not wonder too long
When I see him exposed, do not let my shy eyes close
I want to experience the declaration
My body feels the connection
Give to me that ecstasy, that lingering desire
Make me stagger and my breaths uneasy
That I may leap innocently into his strong embrace and surrender
That is what I dreamed
Drunk on love
It is another day and one leg hurts
My head hurts

Erotic Expressions

He is saying wake up
The sun is shining
Work is calling
Time to go
I am laying there confused, sick and tormented
What did I do? What happened?
I am naked
No make-up on
Hair everywhere
No!
Most are chipper this morning and the birds are singing
I am outside in my car, he is gone, and I am sitting
My mind is on its journey
My manners are a disgrace
My breath is of yesterday
I probably still have slobber crust on my face
I back up in my car, and then I hit the brakes
Let me resolve the situation

CHAPTER 2
Intimate Episodes

Erotic Expressions

Pussy

Infatuation

Stimulation

What brings this temptation and sensation to male beings?

Pussy

Pussy

Pussy

Pussy

Pussy

Pussy

Pussy

The look

Lusterless

Powerless

Disturbed beauty

The smell

Pungent

Sour

Musky

The flavor

Plenty

The taste

Sweet

Salty

The feel

Slippery

Warm

Soft

Rough

Tough

Infatuation

Stimulation

What brings this temptation and sensation to male beings?

Pussy

Pussy

Pussy

Pussy

Pussy

Portal

Birth to all

Give life as the Earth gives life

Beginning

A comforting warm space, the first place before the world will receive you

Often to come back to this place when life mistreats you

Erotic Expressions

Run quickly to this place when people deceive you
Pussy
Infinity
Pussy
Temptation awakens
Pussy
Sensational
Pussy
Femme handicap
Shaven soft kitty
Pretty pussy
Hairy kitty
Like the jungles, search and ye shall find a forbidden fruit
Tempts you to touch
And
Taste
Pussy
Feel it all day
Love it all night
Pussy
Infatuation
Stimulation

What brings this temptation and sensation to male beings?

Pussy

Pussy

Pussy

Pussy

Breast

The suckling of my breast

The squeezing and pulling at my nipples

The massaging of my chest

The warming of my nest

Nerves flutter so

Tickling my womb

Why must you suckle them so?

He replies,

I am infatuated with your

Firm

Shaky

Mounds of soft, smooth flesh

Mounds of soft, smooth flesh

Shaky

Firm

Is my stimulation

Erotic Expressions

Firm

Shaky

Mounds of soft, smooth flesh

Mounds of soft, smooth flesh

Those

Breast

The suckling of my breast

The squeezing and pulling at my nipples

The massaging of my chest

Nerves flutter so

Tickling my womb

Why must you suckle them so?

So little

It is so little

It tickles

Continuous moving orgasms in my middle

It is small, but it is moving them orgasms

Like dancing electricity

It is so little

It tickles

She Speaks a Good Kiss

His thick succulent lips mesmerized her

The curve

The fullness

She could visualize his hard face rested in her hands

His beautiful eyes closed

She would put her lips on his softly

Feeling the heat pass through her

The damp pressure of his desires seeping through

She would rub the tips of her fingers across his scalp

Pushing his face into hers

So divine

Tracing her tongue across the edge of his lips

Lick and pull

Pull and lick

She would open his lips with her prodding tongue

Massage the walls and roof of his mouth with her taste buds

Amuse, jerk, taunt and jostle

The feel of his gyrating tongue tempting to take

Erotic Expressions

over hers
And his thick lips taking hold of her tongue and
suckling it
The sensation would send waves through her
body
Making her go wild
His thick saliva mixing in her thin passion
She would explore his tongue
Kiss him
Explore his mouth
Kiss him
As far, back as his throat
Kiss him
The soft insides of her cheeks
Smitten
Like the fresh pink flesh of a virgin
Her hollow opening constricting
Delicious
She would share his moans
Kiss him
She would share his movement
Kiss him
His energy
The sweet savor of the art

Their tongues graceful
Wild remedy for sensual beings
Passionate in a sensual game
Of erotic foreplay
Kissing
Her voice as striking as a song being swallowed
up by his sensual kisses
His succulent mouth
Colliding with hers
All of her wanting him
In her tight
Fervid place that is pulsating with desire
Awaiting

Dedicated to a man so full of passion in his kiss, a kiss that can awaken the hidden barrier in a woman's spirit and open her heart to the very necessities of warmth that a woman craves.
His kiss is forever, sealed on my lips

Erotic Expressions

Tender Touch

This night of all nights alone

Many silly things on my mind

A bottle of

Sweet tangy wine

Twirling

On my tongue

Going down my throat

Smooth

Slow

In the hot tub I surrender to myself

A shiver

My nipples undulate

It flows to my tummy

Delightful and yummy

It relaxes my mind

Draws the line to temptations of masturbation

I touch myself

An innocent touch

A feather caress

Tightening my legs

My fingers are wet

A silky wet

My hands seem to touch as if they do not belong

to me

Touching my body furiously

Too frantic for a man to believe

My heartbeat shakes against my fingers

The wet slips and drips

I can only close my eyes

Meet ecstasy at its peak

I will make my whole body dance

Motivated by the luscious feeling

Before I bounce and heave

Moan sounds deep within me

Say words of vulgarity to the steam that travels

in and out of me

As I twirl my hips around my hot bath

The sensuality

Spreading

Obsession in my racing fingers

Enthused with rhythm for that orgasm

I closed my legs and hugged them tight

A little shaky

I cried

I Dream

As a woman I dream
Unlike what a man would like to believe
I dream of wild, sensuous things
I dream of rough, painful scenes
I dream of men long, thick, and hard
With strong legs, strong backs, tight ass to toss me around
Against walls
On the bed
Tie me to rails
Lick my body like a snail
Bite my nipples
Scratch words on my belly
Rub all over my body some blackberry jam
Rough, muscled hands with fingers dancing deep in me
Plunging hard
Adventurous
I dream of doctors and physicals
Football players tossing me
Wrestlers head locking me
African herders controlling me
I dream of pastors sanctifying me

Porno masters teaching me
I dream of bikers taking turns riding me 'til I burn
I dream thoughts so damn naughty I am distraught
Nevertheless pleased

Erotic Expressions

Sensual

This day of all days, my mind is drifting

Delayed by the stress of the world

There is no one around to hold me

No one around to scoop up the day

Throw all my stress away

I walk around my house in a dream world

Feeling the night air from my window

Brush against my body like paint

Smelling the musky aroma of incense

Slowly burn off its wood

I, watch the humidified air in my living room space thicken

As my, hot bathwater runs

The loud running of the faucet echoed with the music, like a transparent waterfall in my house

Drip drop drip drop

I fixed a cup of ice tea

I take a sip here and there

Undressing my body to the bare

Letting my clothes fall around me

Slowly

Eventually I surrender to the heat of the bubble bath

The tranquility is moving

It allows my mind to set free its loneliness

Ah, the serenity

The telephone rings and rings and rings

Ignored

Distant music plays

Embracing the moment

In this peaceful place

My dreams on display as I lie here

Thinking of my body wrapped deliciously with yours

Sing Lovers

A moment of comfort a warm touch of another
The feeling is mutual
Lonely, lust and sensuality
These three will create a long night of loving
Sing lovers
Human nature can keep you down
Set your soul at ease in that dark hole that is
fleshy and pink
A warm hug of comfort
It may come in faux but in that moment, it is the
truth
Sing lovers
Enjoy the penetration and elevate the heat
For there are needed calories to burn
An erotic mixture to churn
Sing lovers

Valentine I
(From a man's point of view)

This heart is pulsating
This form is fulsome
This picture is arousing
The thinness in a slender woman's neck
Leading down slightly, to form the fullness in her breast
Like a valentine
The way the hips move and hug onto the thighs
How it spreads away from the arse
Like a valentine
The fresh look of a virgins innocent outline, parted so delicate
Like a rose surrounded by a budding bush to hide its bashful smile and seductive lure
Like a valentine
You are many gifts
A love that will last infinite
Love is not blind because I see you
From the look of your lips
The curve of your hips
The plump lumps in your rump
I feel you

Erotic Expressions

Valentine

Valentine II

(From a woman's point of view)

This heart is pulsating

This form excitingly mannish

This picture is arousing

The smoothness in a fit man

The muscles filling out his form, broadening his shoulders, elevating his chest

His cardiac status in rapture

Like a valentine

The flattening of his back, lifting his ass like that

Lightweight positioning for *Kama sutra*

Like a valentine

The dimple between a man's scrotum, barely creased before the excitement pushes a milky substance up for squirting

Like a valentine

His arms like arrows, flat against her thighs

Locking them down, spreading them wide

Her thighs close to her head as she lifts herself from the bed

Holding him tight and moaning, as he conforms inside

That is a Happy Valentine

Tickles in the Middle

Desire's bursting atomic tickles in the middle
Sculpting pleasure in my own palms
The sheets are long gone
If I were a soprano, I am now a tenor
As breath is silent in my lungs and I am still screaming
Whoever knew that the neck could stretch back this far?
Because I was looking forward when I started and now I am looking back
Only the headboard sees my expression
The tears are so genuine
I am suspended in time
No chorus leaves my mouth now
It is just wide open
My eyes are rolled back into my head viewing the overactive neurons in my brain forming music notes around galaxies
Delicious spasms take course roaming all the ticklish spots
From the contractions of a happy, fervid and

moist orifice

I have become primitive underneath mine own

palms and small fingers

It feels like heaven

Sizzling

Too damn hot

My pigment like melted chocolate

Consume the sweetness; be lost in bliss, even in

the aftertaste

Too damn hot

How long before this puzzle fuses

The temperatures in the U.S.A. are triple digits

Today in Africa it is snowing

My libido is ever growing

My pigment like melted chocolate

Consume the sweetness; be lost in bliss, even in

the aftertaste

That is sensuality showing

He Speaks of a Good Kiss

Her succulent lips mesmerized him

The curve

The fullness

He could envision her soft face rested in his hands

Her beautiful eyes closed

Eyelashes combed down on her cheeks

He would put his lips on her lips

Softly

Feeling the heat pass between them

The damp pressure of her desires seeping through

Just to rub the tips of his fingers across her scalp and feel the softness of her hair flow through

Pushing her face into his

So divine

Tracing his tongue across the edges of her lips

Licking and pulling

Suckling

He would open her lips with his prodding tongue

Massaging the walls and roof of her mouth

Delight

Taunt and caress

Erotic Expressions

The feel of her gyrating tongue tempting to take over
The sensation would send waves through his body
Making him go feral
Her thin saliva mixing with his thick passion
He would explore her tongue
Kiss her
He would explore her mouth
Kiss her
All the way back to her throat
Kiss her
The soft insides of her cheeks
Smitten
Like the fresh pink flesh
Of a virgin
Her hollow opening
Would constrict and he would share her moans
Kiss her
Her energy
Kiss her
The sweet savor of the art
Their tongues graceful
Kiss her

Wild remedy for sensual beings
Passionate in a sensual game
Of erotic foreplay
Kissing
His yearning deep as a growl swallowed up by
her sensual soft kisses
Her succulent mouth
Her warm soft inside
Colliding with his
All of him wanting her
In that bulging place erecting in his pants
Awaiting

Proposal

You brought me to this stage

You asked for my hand on one knee

In front of all these strangers, my body went weak

This is what went through my mind,

When you touch my body and my hunger starts to grow

You are standing there and you do not know that I am

Hungry for your love and all of me is saying YES

The world has disappeared

It is only you and I here on this stage

I am shrouded by your presence

I can hear your breathing

Your anxious heartbeat

Little by little, the talking is fading

Our surroundings inaudible

Something down below

I feel it prickling

I hear it calling

(*make wet pussy sounds with mouth*)

I am dizzy from looking at your lips

It is making that something down below feel

(*Make wet pussy sounds with mouth*)

All of me is saying YES

My pussy is salivating

Labia pouting

Clitoris undulating

Where can your caresses, be found?

Sneak a quick feel if I turn around

Let us leave this stage, like sneaky kids and find a secluded place for a quickie

Do you see the shudder beneath my skin?

I am perspiring from within

 (sing) MMM la dap de dap de dada

You touch my body and the fluids start to flow

I am full of desire and you are standing there not knowing that I am

Thirsty for your love and all of me is saying YES

There is a movie playing in my mind

Stop talking

Im'ma commence to stalking and jump on you

Right on this stage

Do not worry about my beautiful face contorting

All that innocent interior aborting

Right here on this stage I want to ravage you

I have a craving to feed

Go ahead stay on that bent knee

Because something down below is in need

(*Make wet pussy sounds with mouth*)

Every second we are standing here is making me freaky

(Sing) da la de da mmm baby da la de da

My mouth has gone dry I need something inside

A slight indifference to the saying "I'll never do that!"

 I changed my mind I am ready to try and please you

Because you please me and I want to yes I DO

Let me wipe the happy tears from my eyes

Yes I will marry you

Woman
(From a lonely man's point of view)

The rain clouds darken up the sky and the misty air

Its pheromones dispel upon my lonely heart

That yearns for the companionship

Of a woman soft like suede to mine eyes and hands

Eyes large like an owl's constant glare

Lashes like an Asian fan

Dancing and seducing the cheeks

Lips full, and moist

Smile with teeth like pearls

A neck to be caressed kissed and licked

Breast, firm and high

Nipples

Tight orbs of sexual manipulation

The belly

Its soft mound in fever

The hips

In which the clothing falls

Their sway

The dancing way

Those thighs

Erotic Expressions

That hides the treasures

The fervid fountain of delight

The scent of her Lily mouth

Buried inside

The very embodiment of female sexuality

Intense

Predatory

Woman

Heated

(from a lonely man's point of view)

The weather was hot like a kitchen

Humid

Sweaty

Hair thick

Making me itch

She was sweaty too

Her hair was matted across

Her soft features

With perspiration

Clothes clinging to my body

Clothes snug to her body like a second skin

Her long exotic legs

Thick and

Glowing

Parted ever so slightly

Swinging side to side

Like a child gliding in the air on a swing

Her panties

Homely between her vaginal folds

The fragrance of her wet

Pungent fluids

Arousing

Erotic Expressions

Her nipples
Pointing at me
Leaving imprints on her blouse
My manhood in full attention
Rolling up from a lazy twirl
Pushing desperately at my zipper
Rubbing hard against my jeans
Inhale and exhale
Her soft mounds of flesh pulling at her chest
With every breath
Her pretty, little feet in ballerina shoes
I figured I would just go sit next to her and introduce myself
Then she touched my midsection and I tasted her
I did
So earnestly
I could not contain the passion
Beating her flesh with my tongue
Coaxing my palm between her wet thighs
My fingers under the edges of her panties
Into her bare folds of thick soft skin
My tongue lapping at her nipples through her blouse
She was wetting against my palm

I pushed my middle finger inside

I went under her skirt

Snuggled into her middle and I sniffed her as a bull would sniff

A sexy smell

She was so sweet

I slurped her lusty lubricant into my mouth

Fulfilling my dehydrated spirit

Out from its protective skin

She had nowhere to go

Nothing to hold onto

So

I spread her thick thighs

Grabbing her buttocks in my hands

Burying my face in her pubic

Gliding my tongue

Over her rippled flesh

Her breast swaying

With her orgasmic shudders

Moaning like a cat's meow

Every kiss I whispered

Every piece of clothing removed

She became as wild as I

The fire of our desires painful

Erotic Expressions

I begged for copulation
Twisting her labia through my fingers
Yanking down my jeans with the other hand
Grabbing my erect organ
I slid into her
Neither Heaven
Nor hell existed
In this moment
It was a world
Where only I existed
Where I thrust
And I thrust
Myself
Into her fleshy
Heat wave
Repeatedly

FETISHES

It is about that O so good love
                It is about that man's love
It is about that special kind of love
                It is about that special kind of love
It's about that man's love
                It's about that O so good love

Bite me, baby

Pull my nipples wickedly

Slide your tongue to my feet's and wiggle some toes with your teeth

Fetishes

With your large, strong hands, give me a clitoral dance

Let your fingers take a plunge and watch my pussy-opening blow

Fetishes

Rub your long, fat tongue across the edges of my labial lips

I will suck on your fingers, enlarging your member with sufficient blood flow

Fetishes

Choke me and let my larynx scream, I want to aspirate off your steam as you fuck me

Erotic Expressions

Fetishes
Tie my legs to the bed and tickle my clit with spit until I scream fifty times *quit* baby *quit*
Fetishes
Stroke my back pull my hair
Fetishes
Lick my face; let me taste the drool while you dig deeper in my warm vaginal pool
Fetishes
Fuck me hard
Fast hard
Slow hard
Too damn hard
Fuck me hard
Fast hard
Slow hard
Too damn hard
Then look inside my pink pulsating slide and watch it leak
Fetishes
Beat me, oh please, and be nasty and mean, just do not hurt me, bruise me or pick me up and drop me
Fetishes

However we are never done

So much extra fun

Hope the video is on record

Zoom, zoom us a porno, please

Fetishes

Now slide your dick between my breasts and wiggle

Let us do some more nasty shit and giggle

My heartbeats going to give you such a tickle

while my tongue hangs out for the flying drizzle

Fetishes

How about some toys

Fetishes

Maybe you and your boys

Fetishes

Vivid imagination wild stimulation

Orgasm five times

(Smile) Ejaculation

It is about that O so good fucking

    It is about that man and his fucking

It is about that special kind of fucking

    It is about that special kind of fucking

It is about that man and his fucking

    It is about that O so good fucking

Intimate Episodes

Erotic Expressions

! Get To Know!
J.L.Davenport

https://www.facebook.com/author.jldavenport

J.L.Davenport is a spoken word artist, author and songwriter. She speaks about the sensuality we need and the eroticism we seek.

To dare you to open her books and see the imagery in her words would ask you to open a door into her a fantasies and find yourself living them.

Intimate Episodes

www.ingramcontent.com/pod-product-compliance
Lightning Source LLC
Chambersburg PA
CBHW031422040426
42444CB00005B/673